jean
prouvé

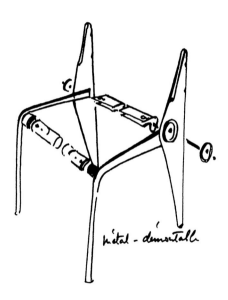

métal - démontable

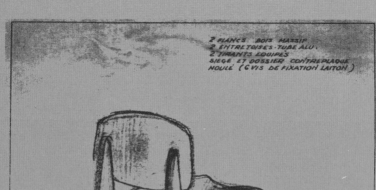

2 FLANCS BOIS MASSIF
2 ENTRETOISES-TUBE ALU.
2 TIRANTS AQUIPES
SIÈGE ET DOSSIER CONTREPLAQUÉ
MOULÉ (6 VIS DE FIXATION LAITON)

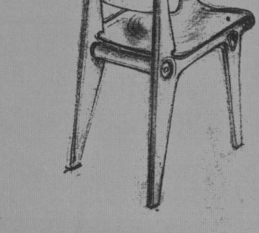

Dessiné :	Vérifié :	N° d'Affaire	ATELIERS JEAN PROUVÉ
Échelle :	Vu :		

CHAISE BOIS DEMONTABLE
N° 301

N° 555 568

Date :

COMPACT DESIGN PORTFOLIO

jean
prouvé

BY PENELOPE ROWLANDS
EDITED BY MARISA BARTOLUCCI + RAUL CABRA

CHRONICLE BOOKS
SAN FRANCISCO

Text copyright © 2002
by Penelope Rowlands.

All images copyright © 2002 by Artist
Rights Society (ARS), New York/ADAGP,
Paris

Design by Raul Cabra, Maxine Ressler &
Betty Ho for Cabra Diseño, San Francisco.

Library of Congress Cataloging-
in-Publication Data available.

ISBN 0-8118-3260-0

Manufactured in China.

Distributed in Canada
by Raincoast Books
9050 Shaughnessy Street
Vancouver, British Columbia V6P 6E5

10 9 8 7 6 5 4 3 2 1

Chronicle Books LLC
85 Second Street
San Francisco, California 94105
www.chroniclebooks.com

FRONT COVER: ANTONY CHAIR, 1950
BACK COVER: WOOD TABLE, 1950
PAGE 1: SKETCH FOR COLLAPSIBLE CHAIR, 1947
PAGE 2: DRAWING FOR COLLAPSIBLE WOOD CHAIR, c. 1950
PAGE 3: COLLAPSIBLE CHAIR IN METAL, 1947
PAGE 6: ALUMINUM WALL PANEL, 1948

ACKNOWLEDGMENTS

Our immense gratitude must be expressed to Catherine Prouvé, the daughter of this design master. Without her determined and unselfish support this book would certainly not have happened. Equally critical to the success of this project were the scholarly tomes provided by Sid Garrison; we cannot thank him enough for his generosity and boundless patience. We are also grateful to Tamotsu Yagi who kindly—and quickly—provided photographs of his extensive collection of Prouvé furniture to illustrate this book. Thanks also go to Cristina Grajales, one of Prouvé's most adoring fans and perceptive scholars, for connecting us with Catherine Prouvé and sharing with the author her keen observations. We also appreciate the patient help of Christine Sorin of the photo archives of the Centre Pompidou for her research work.

And where would we have been without the inspired eyes and graphic talents of Maxine Ressler and Betty Ho at Cabra Diseño? Or without Chronicle's designer Vivien Sung, who trusted us aesthetically and encouraged our play. With regard to encouragement, we were especially fortunate in our cheerleading editor at Chronicle Alan Rapp, who early on championed the idea for this series. He was always at hand with sound editorial and design advice and good humor.

PHOTO CREDITS

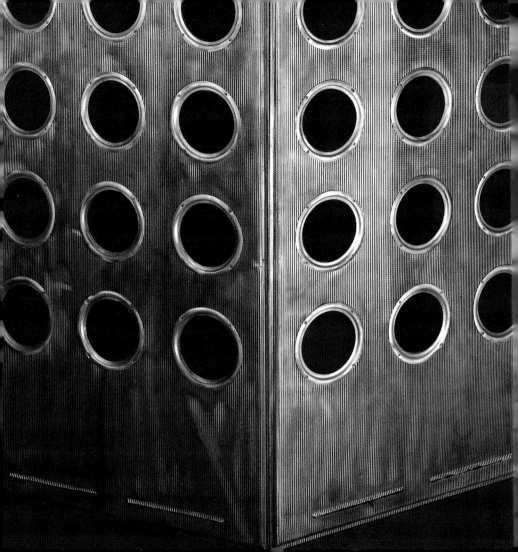

Jean Prouvé

Visionary Humanist   By Penelope Rowlands

"He combines the soul of an engineer with that of an architect," Le Corbusier once said of Jean Prouvé. Technically, he was neither. Prouvé was a "constructeur"— quite simply, a builder—one who happened to work with some of the most forward-thinking architects of his day, creating with them miraculous structures of sheet steel and other then-daring materials. In his parallel work as a furniture designer he was equally audacious, turning out pieces that still look crisply modern sixty or seventy years after he first brought them to life. We can, and do, learn from them still.

"It's a very rational aesthetic, a mixture of the biomorphic and rationalist," says R. Craig Miller, curator of architecture, design, and graphics at the Denver Art Museum. **"Prouvé sort of burst forward with a fresh vision,"** he adds. **"I think of him as the central French designer in the immediate post–World War II period."** Examples of this "bursting-forward" quality abound in Prouvé's work. For a man described by all as shy and self-effacing, the designs he produced had personality to spare. A rounded elevator cage, made in the 1930s of glistening stainless steel, resembles a futuristic coffee pot. An entrance lodge to a factory, also made in the 1930s, seems to mix a Boy Scout sensibility with a Japanese one.

Sometimes his furniture took on tasks that no other pieces had done before. Needing light, an architecture student could draw at a long wooden table, which Prouvé designed with Charlotte Perriand, working by the glow of a futuristic light fixture that encircled it. Half a dozen children, sharing a metal dining table at summer camp, could store their cloth napkins at the side of the table in six small holes made for that purpose. Most of Prouvé's furniture designs were conceived for institutional use; as such, the surviving pieces often have a beaten-up look. Still, they manage to seem forever young.

Paradoxically, for a man whose work is now so widely known, in his lifetime Prouvé's genius was rather less apparent. He once said that he had a "2-CV way of thinking," cannily equating himself with the Deux Chevaux, the classic, dirt-cheap two-horsepower French automobile that, like so much of Prouvé's work, manages to be visually appealing, deeply modest, and practical all at once. He described himself as "haunted by a passion to build." As the French scholar Catherine Coley has pointed out, "Only construction, the surface of materials and the fullness of volumes, engaged him completely."

And he was engaged at every level. Prouvé is famous for having once said, "The problems to be solved [in the making of furniture] are just as complex as those to be solved in large construction projects." Both his buildings and furniture evidenced brilliant solutions. Some borrowed from other worlds, such as a 1930s table that features a rubber top stretched across supports of nickeled steel, a solution clearly lifted from aircraft construction. (A man who loved the ingenuity of the modern age, Prouvé adored both planes and cars.) Conference tables, balanced on what he called "airplane wing" bases, look poised for take off. Even his grander furniture, such as the regal, angular 1950 Présidence desk, is deeply utilitarian. **The goal of most of these pieces is mass manufacture, easy living, ingenious practicality.** Everything about his work encourages flexibility: a pioneer in the use of folded metal, Prouvé pinched the tubing on his chair legs so the pieces would stack; he made others that folded, so they could be tucked away when not in use.

Made for the masses, Prouvé's furniture is now coveted by a small but growing group of collectors, most of them decidedly nonproletarian, such as movie star Brad Pitt, art dealer Larry Gagosian, and clothing designer Marc Jacobs. Once abundant in Parisian flea markets, his furniture has become increasingly rare—and increasingly sought after. "We're having great difficulty finding pieces, even the most basic Jean Prouvé side chair," laments Christina Grajales, director of 1950, a New York furniture gallery. (Its owner, Tony Delorenzo, is largely credited with bringing Prouvé's work to an American audience.) "Once I had three hundred of them! At this point I have two." According to Grajales, the secret to the furniture's appeal is no secret at all: "The pieces are so beautiful. The proportions, the lines, are so perfect."

Prouvé grew up surrounded by art and music. His father, Victor, was a noted craftsman and engraver who also dabbled in the fine arts, both painting and sculpture, and his mother, Marie, was a musician. Prouvé was said to be always drawing. "It was a very specific artistic environment," says Catherine Prouvé, his youngest daughter. "I always heard my father say that his education was art. As a child, he worked side by side with his father."

"I was born at the École de Nancy," Prouvé once said. This group, officially known as L'Alliance Provinciale des Industries d'Art, was founded in 1901—the very year that Jean was born. Founded by Émile Gallé, the noted glassblower and son of a prominent local industrialist, the École de Nancy aimed to reform industrial production, bringing a more craftsmanlike approach to industry and vice versa. Although it was essentially an economic alliance, one that united local craftsmen like Prouvé's father, it also had a pedagogic function: workers were trained in techniques from design to production. Above all, they were committed to the new. "Be of your time," Victor Prouvé used to exhort his son. With only fleeting exceptions early in his career, he was.

To Prouvé, members of the École de Nancy were revolutionaries. "They had assembled at Lorraine open minds from every discipline," he said. "[They had] everything they needed to proceed efficiently toward creating an art of their epoch. I was inculcated with one of their abiding principles, that man must not allow himself to plagiarize. He is on this earth to create." Gallé, who was Jean Prouvé's godfather, summed up the prevailing principles: "Healthy construction must answer to its location and materials. The execution must be as simple and as logical as possible. [It] should not be masked by anything; it should always be apparent."

The goal was "daily humanism"; one should live and create with humility. It's perhaps for this reason that, despite an exceptional body of work and the fact that he died only recently in 1984, Prouvé seems to have left a fairly light impression on the earth. If he maintained a low profile, it may have been in part for philosophical reasons: the work of the group was what mattered most.

Prouvé was one of seven children raised in financially precarious circumstances. As the eldest son, he was in charge of a gang of younger siblings. He had hoped to train as an engineer, but couldn't for financial reasons. Around 1916, when still a teenager, he was apprenticed to Émile Robert, an ironworker with a small studio in Enghien. Later he went to Paris to work under Hungarian ironsmith Adalbert Szabo. In 1923, with the help of a family friend, he opened his first workshop, back home in Nancy. "He was only twenty-three," his daughter says. "But a friend of the family must have seen what he could do, so he said, 'Tell me what you need to get things started, for machinery and things.' My father came up with a very low figure, too low, and this friend then doubled it." **Prouvé referred to this first workshop as an "atelier," a term he would use for all his facilities, including factories, both in Paris and Nancy. He ran them on a socialist model, one that assumed an equality between workers**

and management. Tellingly, he was particular about what he called his employees, referring to them as *compagnons*, a word that seems perfectly Prouvé–esque, since it means both "companion" and "craftsman."

Prouvé's first commissions were in wrought iron and were heavily influenced by Art Nouveau, a style then still in demand. Soon, though, he revealed his Nancian roots, refusing imitation, seeking out newer forms both in his furniture and, later in the 1930s, in his buildings. He was a pioneer of industrialization, endlessly toying with new materials and different methods of manufacturing. He was, for instance, one of the first building designers to use folded sheet steel, a material he loved in part for its unexplored potential. And while other architects used semifinished products, such as pressed steel, Prouvé manufactured the folded steel himself.

By 1924, he was developing his first prototypes of furniture, including adjustable armchairs and folding chairs. **"I couldn't be satisfied with arched steel tubing," Prouvé later stated, referring to the preferred material of such Modernists as Le Corbusier, Mies van der Rohe, and Marcel Breuer. "It was sheet steel that inspired me—folded, pressed, ribbed, then soldered."** Phillipe Jousse, a longtime dealer in Prouvé's furniture, believes he also liked folded steel because of its greater strength. If style wasn't Prouvé's first concern, it was certainly a by-product. "There's a Prouvé style, even if he didn't want one," Jousse contends.

In the early 1920s, Prouvé met Le Corbusier, Pierre Jeanneret, and Charlotte Perriand, with whom he would later collaborate on furniture, as well as Robert Mallet-Stevens, who commissioned him to do a large protective grill for a *hôtel particulier*. Prouvé designed a supremely geometric creation that resembled wrought iron but was in fact made of polished steel. Not long afterward, Mallet-Stevens founded UAM, or L'Union des Artistes Modernes, after an ideological schism divided the long-reigning Société des Artistes Décorateurs, which held to a much more decorative aesthetic. Along with Le Corbusier, Charlotte Perriand, and Pierre Chareau, Prouvé became one of UAM's first members. "The machine should be the instrument of a return to craftsmanship as a way to regenerate the industry of art" was the group's credo, and it could as easily have been penned by the founders of the École de Nancy. Both organizations believed in pragmatic, innovative solutions to design problems, saw art as pure form, and emphasized the importance of materials.

In 1925, Prouvé married a former student of his father's, named Madeleine Schott. The couple would eventually have six children, though one died in infancy. "He was very paterfamilias," recalls his daughter Catherine, describing a family life that bore more than a passing resemblance to the household in which Jean himself had been raised. "It was very lively," she adds. **There were always a lot of people at the house. Everyone was welcome to come and live as we did. We'd move over at the table so our friends could eat with us." Those who came were a mixed, happy bag, as she tells it, from gangs of cousins to "people like Le Corbusier."**

In marrying Madeleine, Prouvé acquired a powerful ally. "She was very important in her support for him," says Catherine. "She believed in him enormously." It was after his marriage that Prouvé really took off as a designer, creating all manner of things, from elevator cages to door handles, at one point even drawing up plans for a car.

His early furniture designs show signs of the almost effortless innovation that would become his trademark, such as a one-of-a-kind adjustable armchair made of folded steel from 1930. Reminiscent of a wheelchair, it has huge semicircular armrests that arch from front to back.

Prouvé first came up with what must be one of his most famous pieces, the standard chair, a sidechair characterized by an aeronautic-looking pair of rear legs, in the early 1930s. He would make variations of it for decades. "It has a real strength about it," Craig Miller says of this chair, referring, presumably, to both its sturdiness and its design. Untold numbers of students would sit through classes in these chairs, which were ordered in quantity by the Lycée at Metz, the University of Nancy, and numerous other institutions. By now iconic, this molded chair is rooted in practicality, with back legs that are wider than the front ones for durability and balance. Factory made, like all Prouvé's furniture, they still managed to have a crafted quality. "You can almost sense that they've been hand finished," adds Miller. Prouvé made the first of these chairs in folded sheet metal with a padded seat. Over the years, the design became more streamlined. By the mid-1930s he produced its most famous incarnation with a curved plywood seat and back. During World War II, when metal was scarce, he fabricated the chair entirely from wood. An armchair version, with arms growing directly out of its steel back legs, was made in the 1950s. Other versions were manufactured in aluminum. Still others folded or collapsed.

By 1931, Prouvé had opened "Les Ateliers J. Prouvé S.A.," a larger facility in Nancy with more than forty employees and much new equipment, including more powerful machines for folding sheet metal. (Five years later, Prouvé would acquire an even larger press.) "It was the real beginning of sheet metal construction," says Jean-Marie Glatigny, a former collaborator of Prouvé's (as quoted by Peter Sulzer, the architectural scholar who is the author of an ongoing catalogue raisonné of Prouvé's work). Although the design historian Martin Eidelberg refers to a prevailing "antagonism to metal [in France] in the 1930s," Prouvé was clearly immune. Metal was used copiously in his furniture that was shown at UAM's salon in the fall of 1930, and it's tempting to think that, for Prouvé and other confirmed Modernists, part of the appeal of this material lay in the fact that it resisted ornamentation. It couldn't be worked or carved, as wood had been—particularly by the French—for centuries. The national tendency to Roccoco could finally be put to rest. **By contrast, metal almost invited streamlining, which attracted Prouvé, who was always interested in how the engineering techniques used in planes and cars could be transferred to buildings.** Once he commented, cryptically, that "If we made airplanes like we make houses, they wouldn't fly!"

Prouvé distinguished himself from fellow designers such as Le Corbusier by wanting, even insisting, on keeping the craftsmanlike quality of his work apparent. His furniture, while factory made, often had visible hesitations and reworkings. It reminds you that, in a sense, Prouvé was making it up as he went along. Although both he and Le Corbusier thought that mass manufacturing was the ideal, Prouvé's work—intentionally, you sense—never entirely looked the part. While Le Corbusier was enamored of his vision, contemplating the beauty of skyscrapers and futuristic cityscapes, Prouvé remained firmly planted on the earth. No matter what new or experimental techniques he brought to his furniture and structures, you can always see the human hand at work.

At the latest factory in Nancy, Prouvé perfected a new way of working. On one side of the plant, plans were drawn and sheet metal was manufactured; on the other, furnishings and other objects were assembled. Even when designing prefabricated buildings, Prouvé followed the protocol he used for furniture: he'd sketch, make prototypes, then modify his designs—all before drawing actual plans. Sometimes this process was abbreviated, with prototypes being modified even as they were being made. The nature of manufacturing seldom lends itself to spontaneity—except, apparently, at the Ateliers Prouvé. **Prouvé himself worked with the fluidity of a sculptor or artisan, always open to revisions as they came along. The extraordinary, almost unbelievable fact is that he did so in a factory context.**

"What is the material thinking?" Prouvé would ask himself as he sat down to design. He encouraged his workers in a similar approach. "He taught me to feel materials," Antti Lovag, a Hungarian-born architect and former employee has written. "One day he gave me an awning to design and I tried [but unsuccessfully]. Then he appeared with a piece of sheet metal and said to me, 'Touch that. See how it reacts to different maneuvers. Then draw it.'"

In the 1930s, huge furniture commissions began coming Prouvé's way from hospitals, schools, universities, and other institutions. Prototypes were made and reworked. From this period dates what is probably Prouvé's first desk design, a semicircular, folded sheet steel frame with a laminate top and a base of stainless-steel plate. His first dormitory furniture for the University at Nancy was also created during this time. Prouvé won this commission by competition, and years later would brag that his was the only furniture used in these dormitories that had endured. Many of these pieces, including the camp-style bed, with its combined bookshelf and headboard, have long since become classics. Other versions, such as a bed with an "air-circulation headboard," made for the sick room at the École Nationale Professionelle at Metz, reveal Prouvé's tireless innovation. Indeed, examples of his radical invention are legion, among them a cradle fashioned from stainless-steel strips, and a 1930s-era modular school desk and chair with large wheels at its base.

Some of Prouvé's earliest architectural projects were revolutionary, including a bus station designed in 1933 to be built in the La Villette section of Paris. Although this project was never built, it was nonetheless historic: it was the the first building designed entirely of folded sheet metal. According to Prouvé's daughter, Catherine, Prouvé came to designing buildings in increments, beginning with the fanciful elevator cages he'd come up with in the 1920s. "He started little by little. He never did anything until he had mastered things. He made a lot of construction elements; then, little by little, he came to whole buildings."

With the UAM architects Eugene Beaudouin and Marcel Lods, with whom he would work again and again, Prouvé created the Aéro-club Roland-Garros, a rectangular building of sheet steel—entirely prefabricated at the Prouvé workshops—that was designed and built within a year (1935–36). **"We had to invent everything, and we did so with great boldness," Prouvé later told Sulzer. The daring of this design is such that photographs of it still look contemporary today.** By 1936, Lods had made use of that inventiveness in one of their most important commissions: the Maison du Peuple in Clichy, which was completed in 1939 (and extensively renovated in the late 1990s). Prouvé was responsible for both the design and construction of this building, which featured what is said to be the first curtain wall constructed entirely of sheet steel. (Its distinctive glass-and-metal awning was attached to the structure with folded sheet steel brackets.) This was a complex structure that contained a market area, auditorium, cinema, and various promenades and shops. The auditorium was distinguished by an operable floor and partition system and retractable balustrade. When Frank Lloyd Wright visited the building, he is said to have exclaimed: "We haven't gotten this far in the United States!"

During this period, Prouvé came up with some imaginative solutions to housing, most notably a prototype for a prefabricated house, designed with Beaudouin and Lods, that was a hit at the 1939 Salon des Arts Ménagers. Made of solid and sheet steel, this structure had a caravan-like appearance, which seems perfectly apt, given that, according to a description written for the Salon, it was "meant to provide holiday accommodation that is comfortable enough to make for a pleasant stay even when there is continuous bad weather." (With war impending in Europe, this, among other Prouvé projects, was not produced.) Another appealing prefab house was a 1939 vacation home; perched on stilts, it could have a steel or pine-log exterior, depending on the whim of its owners.

The war would change Prouvé's furniture, most obviously in the materials he used. With metal scarce, he turned to wood. A group of typing desks he produced at this time, including one with a drop-front filing drawer and perfectly tapered legs, offers ample evidence that his designs were constantly evolving. So, too, were his other activities. In 1940, Prouvé joined the Résistance. In recognition of his service, after the war, he was named Mayor of Nancy, a largely symbolic post he held for one year.

The housing shortage that followed the war enabled Prouvé to explore his interest in prefabrication. Predictably, he was intrigued by the idea of "social housing," of creating quick, easy living solutions for the masses. With the help of specialized workers, some of his designs could be assembled in a day. While Prouvé aimed for ever-greater standardization, manufacturing prefabricated pieces that were interchangeable, there was nothing bland about the work he produced.

A story told by his daughter Catherine nicely demonstrates the ease—and sometimes joy—that prefabrication allowed. In 1946, Prouvé was contemplating how and where to send his family on vacation (he was too involved in his projects to join them), when he remembered that, stashed away in his atelier, he still had pieces of a prefab house he'd designed for refugees. Soon, Madeleine Prouvé, some of her children, and parts of the house were on their way to Brittany by train. (Other parts, and children, followed in a truck, accompanied by a clutch of Prouvé-designed furniture and two workmen to help with assembly.) "We spent two months in that house," Catherine remembers. "I have wonderful memories of it." With supreme, Prouvéian practicality, once the object was achieved—a great summer vacation—the house was sold, its now-almost-priceless furniture distributed among friends.

The same year, Prouvé's ateliers moved to a larger facility in the Nancian suburb of

Maxéville. Its operations grew accordingly: more *compagnons* were hired and an even greater level of industrialization achieved. The next year, part of the atelier was officially consecrated to furniture. These years saw some of the greatest of Prouvé's achievements in this domain, including the famous combined shelving unit and bench that he designed in 1952 with Charlotte Perriand for the Maison de Tunisie at the Cité Universitaire in Paris. According to Catherine Prouvé, this famous piece originated with Charlotte Perriand, who, years before, had designed a wooden library unit with Pierre Jeanneret. Eventually, she asked Prouvé to come up with "something open and in metal," as Catherine Prouvé puts it. Prouvé and Perriand collaborated on the piece, then turned to the painter Sonia Delaunay—known for her chromatic studies—to supply its color scheme. At Maxéville, forty of these were made out of mahogany and enameled pine, with sliding doors in sheet aluminum.

During this period, Prouvé became increasingly intrigued by aluminum, which soon supplanted his beloved sheet steel in his work. It must have seemed a natural, then, when Studal, the commercial arm of the French national aluminum company, came along and offered a welcome influx of cash to Prouvé's operation in return for the exclusive right to sell its construction elements. By 1952, they had acquired majority control of the ateliers; by the following year, the entire enterprise had slipped from Prouvé's hands. Precipitously, Prouvé had entered what he'd later call "a period without joy."

Under Studal's control, the atelier was reconfigured, so that designing and manufacturing became separate processes, rather than two halves of an organic whole, as they had been, always, for Prouvé. It was not long before the quality of the work emerging from the ateliers declined. Prouvé's long-held goal of finding the "ideal industrial way of production" would never be achieved. "The politics of our ateliers are light-years away from the principles that brought us to success" was Prouvé's mournful and accurate assessment before he quit the studio for good in 1955. "It's the end of the model I inherited from the École de Nancy."

Improbably, some of Prouvé's best work was still to come. In 1953, he developed some extraordinary aluminum guillotine windows for a building on the Square Mozart in Paris. The windows were covered with an innovative set of shutters: they slid up or down to block the light, and could open out at an angle, the way Italian ones do, to let in air. These elements weren't just practical, they provided interest, too, "a constant visual animation," as scholar Catherine Coley puts it. In a seemingly changeless haute-bourgeois Paris neighborhood, the facade was constantly in flux, altering intriguingly, from minute to minute, day to day.

While Prouvé stopped working on furniture in the mid-1950s, and no longer turned out large-scale building projects, he still produced masterpieces, including his own house in Nancy, which he built just after his departure from the ateliers in 1954. Ironically, Prouvé's association with Studal gave him the means to create the house he and Madeleine had hoped to build for years. It also offered a way "to maintain hope," as Catherine Prouvé puts it, after his disastrous association with that company. "Numerous studies had been made for the house," she adds, "notably with aluminum sheds, which were being studied at that point in the factory." True to form, Prouvé used a simple, logical floor plan, along with a double-curved roof. Beyond that, he improvised, making use of leftover stock from his factory. "We all took part in the construction," says Catherine, recalling how the house was built one summer with family and friends. The city of Nancy bought the home in 1991, and it's now in use as a private residence.

"There was an exceptional atmosphere in the house when it was inhabited by my parents," she recalls. "The paintings it contained were by Victor Prouvé, the furniture was Prouvé furniture, with the exception of a very beautiful table that was a gift of Pierre Jeanneret. The curtains had been woven by my sister Simone. There were knits by my mother, photographs and drawings by grandchildren, and lots of music. It was extremely warm, alive, and natural."

At around this time, working closely with the engineer Michel Hugonet, Prouvé conceived of the Centenary Pavilion of Aluminum. A striking structure, held together, appropriately enough, by posts of extruded aluminum, it was the first important building he designed entirely after the close of his ateliers. In 1955, having moved to Paris to work (he returned to Nancy and his family each weekend), Prouvé founded Jean Prouvé Constructions, a small company set up to research housing solutions. The goal was to create easy-to-assemble, inexpensive structures to serve as social housing. Perhaps the most brilliant of these was the house of Abbé Pierre, a near-mythical French figure known for his charity toward the poor. **Made of sleek, almost organically molded wood, this prefabricated structure had, in the Prouvé manner, an almost accidental beauty. It was acclaimed by Le Corbusier as "the most beautiful house I know."** Certainly, it must also have been one of the easiest to install: it was put up on Paris's Left Bank, on the quai Alexandre III, in only seven hours, in the middle of a Paris workday, with all its implied traffic and chaos. Although acclaimed by the public, this house, for various bureaucratic reasons, never went beyond this one elegant prototype.

In 1957, Prouvé took over the buildings department of the Compagnie Industrielle de Matériel de Transport (CIMT). By the following year, CIMT was the leader of the construction of *façades légères,* or prefabricated facades, for institutional buildings. The sheet aluminum or stamped panels that made up these facades could be easily applied to almost any structure, particularly ones made of concrete. Prouvé remained active in this capacity for years. His curiosity and openness to new forms never diminished with age. He was devising new building systems well into his sixties, and after retiring from CIMT, he opened a practice in Paris as a consulting engineer. Age didn't diminish his audacity: in 1970, working with architects Reiko Hayama and Serge Binotto, Prouvé created circular wood-and-steel structures that would serve as environmentally sensitive mountain chalets. In his later years, he even experimented with the idea of creating inflatable buildings.

Curiously, though, his most visible legacy is one he didn't design himself. Prouvé was the president of the jury in the 1971 competition that selected Richard Rogers and Renzo Piano as the architects for the Centre Pompidou, the French National Museum of Modern Art. This wondrous, still-daring inside-out-looking tangle of colored pipes revitalized the heart of Paris and still draws millions of visitors to this day.

On a smaller scale, and perhaps most insistently, Prouvé's furniture continues to inspire. "After you've settled down with him, there's nowhere else to go," says collector Susie Tompkins. Prouvé's furniture, she says, has lessons to impart; she credits its unassuming, almost proletarian elegance with helping her to live in a more down-to-earth way. **"It's very serviceable and very beautiful at the same time,"** as she puts it. Others have remarked on a moral component in Prouvé's furniture. "He was such a humane person," observes Christina Grajales. "He had great integrity. I think that translates into the pieces." Paradoxically, wonderfully, it does. In this way, a century after it was founded, the École de Nancy lives on.

JEAN PROUVÉ, 1955

Commissioned by Robert Mallet-Stevens to make a large protective grill for a *hôtel particulier*, Prouvé designed a supremely geometric creation of polished steel.

FAR LEFT AND TOP LEFT: LAMP STANDS, MID-1920s

BOTTOM LEFT: WROUGHT IRON DOOR FOR THE
BANQUE D'ALSACE-LORRAINE, PARIS, 1929

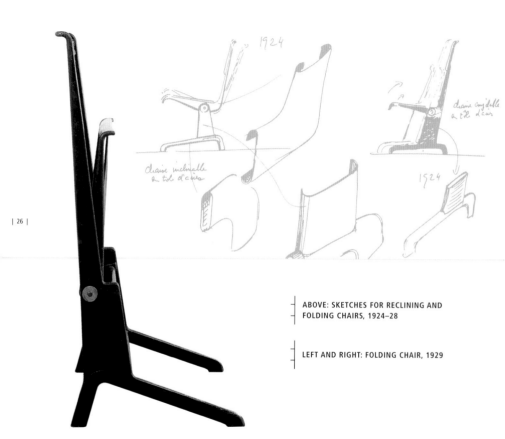

chaise inclinable
en tôle d'acier

chaise comfortable
en tôle d'acier

1924

1924

ABOVE: SKETCHES FOR RECLINING AND
FOLDING CHAIRS, 1924–28

LEFT AND RIGHT: FOLDING CHAIR, 1929

CITÉ ARMCHAIR FRAME AND DRAWING, 1933

LEFT: CITÉ ARMCHAIR, 1933

FOLLOWING PAGES: PROUVÉ FAMILY HOME, NANCY, 1954

Je soussigné Prouvé jean
Déclare avoir cédé à Monsieur
Kers Stopp pour la somme de 2000 Fs
— deux mille francs — un fauteuil
métallique de grand repos dont
ci contre un croquis

Fait à Nancy le 15 juillet 1981

Prouvé

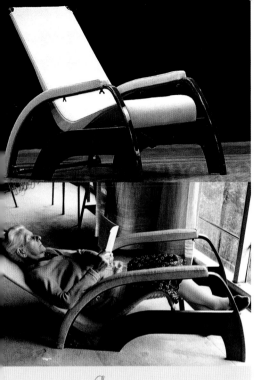

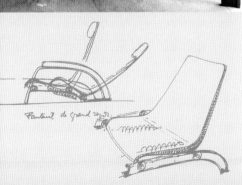

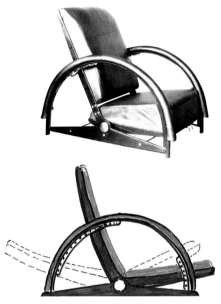

FAR LEFT: RECLINING METAL ARMCHAIR, 1945

LEFT: RECLINING ARMCHAIR, 1930

ABOVE: RECLINING ADJUSTABLE ARMCHAIR, 1930

VISITOR ARMCHAIR, 1942

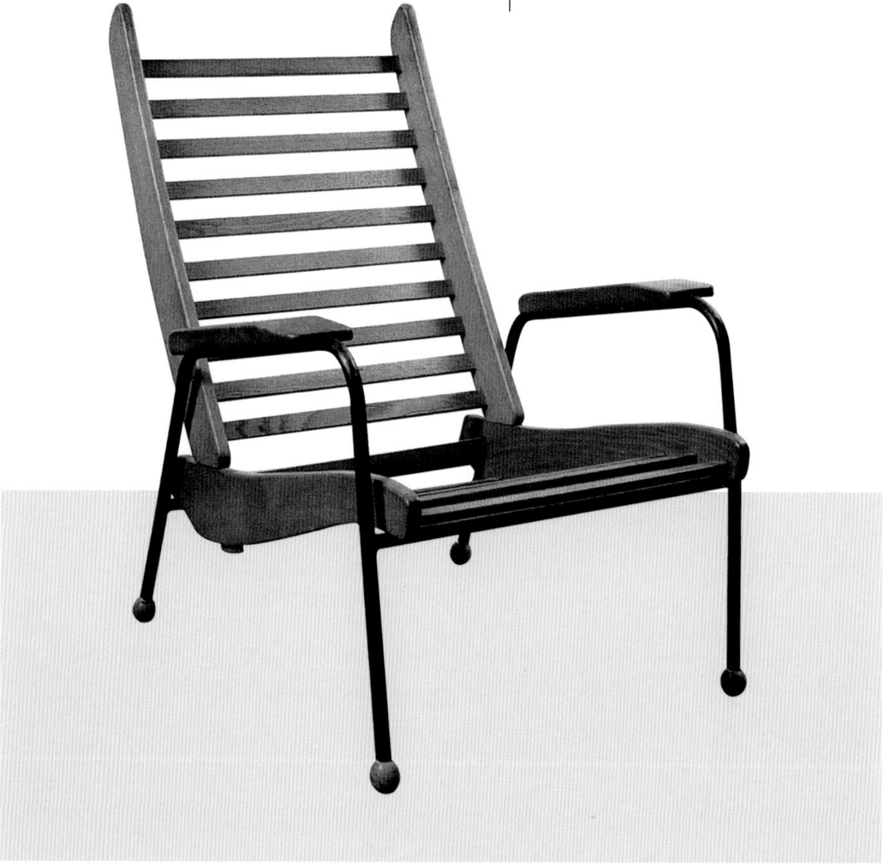

"It was sheet steel that inspired me—folded, pressed, ribbed, then soldered."

COLLAPSIBLE CHAIR, 1947

STANDARD CHAIR, c. 1950

WOOD CHAIR, 1942

CHILD'S SCHOOL CHAIR, c. 1937

COMPASS ARMCHAIR, c. 1950

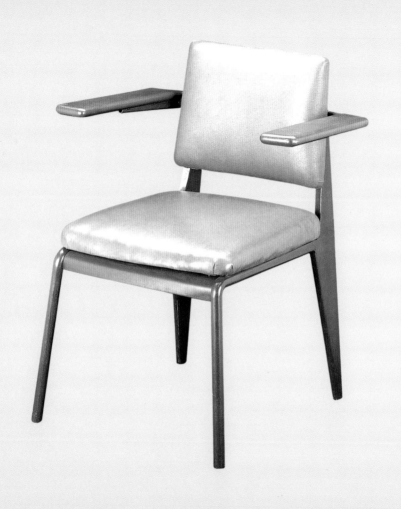

BRIDGE DIRECTOR ARMCHAIRS, c. 1950

PRESIDENTIAL BRIDGE ARMCHAIRS, c. 1950

ANTONY CHAIR, 1950

MEXICAN (1953) AND TUNISIAN (1952)
BOOKSHELVES, COFFEE TABLE (1950), AND
ANTONY CHAIR WITH ROCKER BASE (c. 1950s)

BANQUETTE, 1954

JEAN PROUVÉ AND STOOL, c. 1950

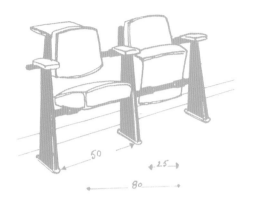

AMPHITHEATRE BANQUETTE, 1956

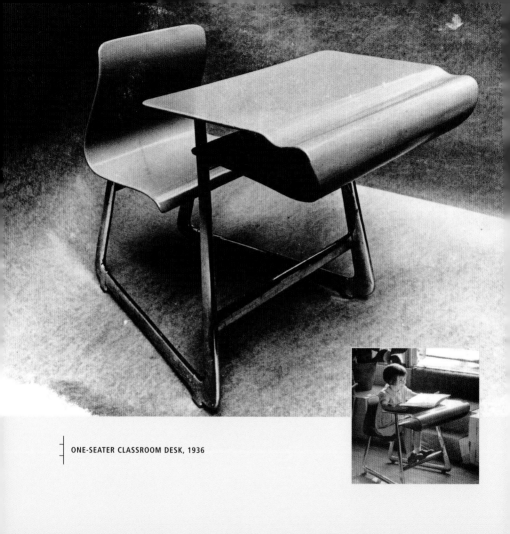

ONE-SEATER CLASSROOM DESK, 1936

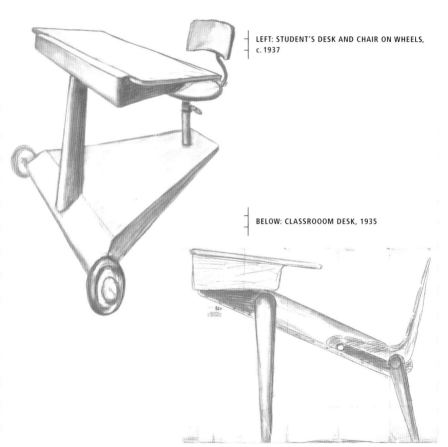

LEFT: STUDENT'S DESK AND CHAIR ON WHEELS,
c. 1937

BELOW: CLASSROOOM DESK, 1935

| 53 |

DESK AND CHAIR FOR THE UNIVERSITY OF NANCY, 1933

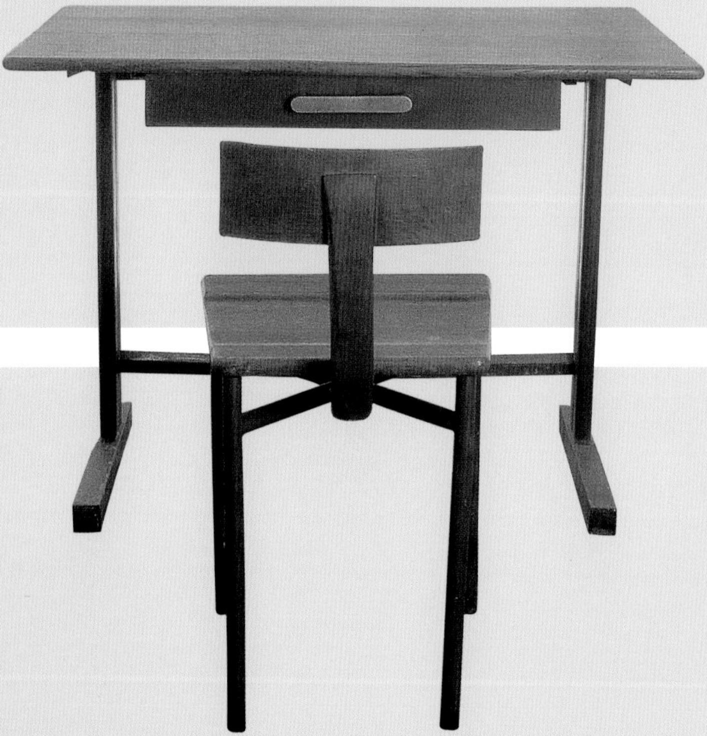

TOP LEFT: CLASSROOOM DESK, 1935

TOP RIGHT: TWO-SEATER CLASSROOM TABLE, 1935

RIGHT: CLASSROOM DESK AND SEAT, c. 1930S–1940s

Prouvé wanted, even insisted, on keeping the craftsmanlike quality of his work apparent. His furniture,
while factory made, often had visible hesitations and
reworkings.

BUREAU COMPASS DESK, 1948

ROUNDED COMPASS DESK WITH TWO DRAWERS,
1958

GREAT WING COMPASS DESK, 1958

PORTABLE HOUSE, 1942

LARGE COMPASS DESK, c. 1950

RIGHT: PRESIDENTIAL DESK, 1950
CROSSOVER: PLAN FOR PRESIDENTIAL DESK,
c. 1950

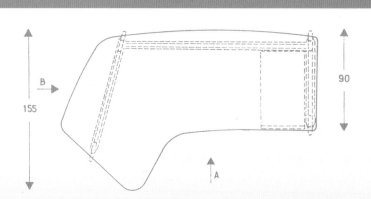

155

B

90

A

| 61 |

170

240

DINING TABLE, c. 1940–45

COFFEE TABLE , c. 1940–45

PEDESTAL TABLE, 1951

Plateau

Armature métallique

Pieds bois

WOOD TABLE, 1950
RIGHT: TABLE DETAIL

TABLE WITH LACQUERED ALUMINUM TOP AND
BENT STEEL BASE, 1950

FOLLOWING PAGES: (LEFT) WOOD TABLE, 1951;
(RIGHT) EXHIBITION OF JEAN PROUVÉ'S FURNISH-
INGS, GALERIE JOUSSE SEGUIN, PARIS, 1994

"The problems to be solved [in the making of furniture] are just as complex as those to be solved in large construction projects," Prouvé observed. Both his buildings and furniture evidenced brilliant solutions.

WORKSHOP TABLE, 1950

FOLLOWING PAGES: CAFETERIA AT THE CACHAT SPRING, EVIAN, 1955–56

A man who loved the ingenuity of the modern age, Prouvé adored both planes and cars. Conference tables, balanced on what he called "airplane wing" bases, look poised for take off.

TRAPEZE CONFERENCE TABLE, 1954

TABLE WITH BUILT-IN LIGHT, 1953

GRANIPOLI TABLE, 1939

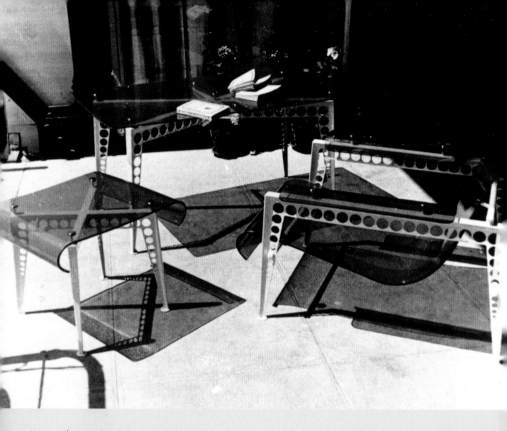

PLEXIGLAS-AND-STEEL ARMCHAIR AND TABLE
FOR INTERNATIONAL EXHIBITION, 1937

SKETCH OF EXHIBITION HALL, LILLE, 1950

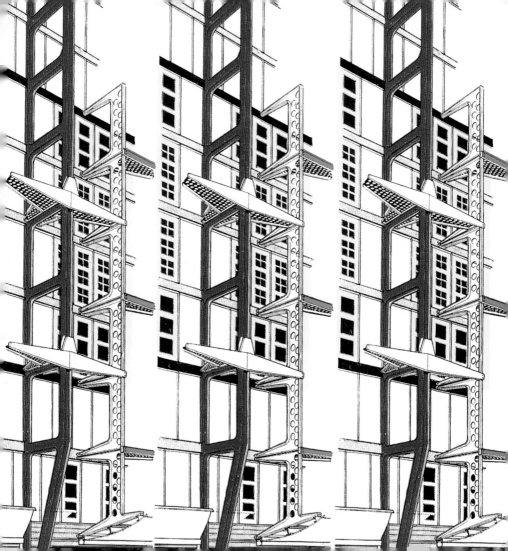

STUDENT HOUSING FOR THE CITÉ UNIVERSITAIRE
IN NANCY, 1933

BED, 1938

"The goal of most of these pieces is mass manufacture, easy living, ingenious practicality."

ASYMMETRICAL BED WITH BUILT-IN DRAWER, 1950

SWING JIB LAMP, 1950

STANDARD CHAIRS (1950) AND TABLE WITH
BENT STEEL BASE AND SAND-BLASTED GLASS
TOP (1945)

SHIFTING FACADE OF THE MOZART SQUARE
APARTMENT HOUSE, 1953

MEXICAN BOOKCASE, DESIGNED WITH
CHARLOTTE PERRIAND, 1953

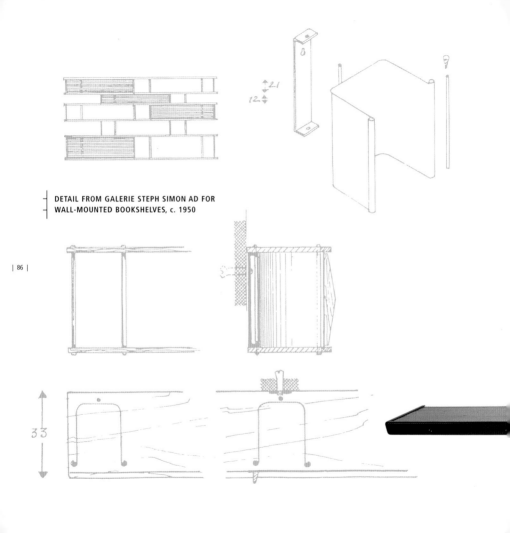

DETAIL FROM GALERIE STEPH SIMON AD FOR
WALL-MOUNTED BOOKSHELVES, c. 1950

2.1

12

33

WALL-MOUNTED BOOKSHELVES, DESIGNED WITH
CHARLOTTE PERRIAND, c. 1950s

TUNISIAN BOOKCASE, DESIGNED WITH CHARLOTTE
PERRIAND AND SONIA DELAUNAY, 1952

CABINET, 1949

WARDROBE, c. 1945

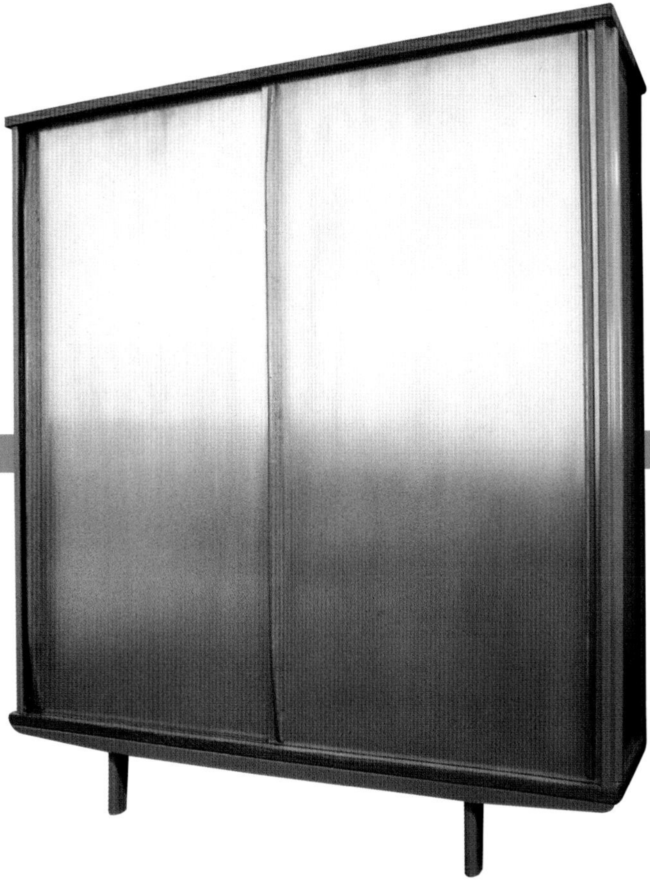

He described himself as "haunted by a passion to

build." As the French scholar Catherine Coley has

pointed out, "Only construction, the surface of

materials and the fullness of volumes, engaged him

completely."

JEAN PROUVÉ

JEAN PROUVÉ BIOGRAPHY

1901	Born April 8 in Paris to Victor Prouvé, a noted craftsman, and his musician wife, Marie. Grows up in Nancy, France
1918–1919	Apprenticed to the art metal worker, Émile Robert
1919–1921	Apprenticed to the art metal worker, Adalbert Szabo
1923	Opens his own atelier in Nancy
1923–26	Makes his first furniture, including such classics as the chair with folding seat and reclining armchair, both in sheet steel; the aeronautic table; and the armchair of sheet steel with leather arm rests. In Paris, meets Le Corbusier, Pierre Jeanneret, Charlotte Perriand, and Robert Mallet-Stevens
1925	Marries Madeleine Schott, a student of his father's
1927	Makes the armchair Cité Universitaire
1929	Receives first patent for a movable partition wall
1930	Becomes a founding member of the Union des Artistes Modernes (UAM); establishes Les Ateliers J. Prouvé S.A., a larger facility in Nancy with more than forty employees and much new equipment, including machines for folding sheet steel
1931	Makes doors and furniture for the University of Nancy
1935	Makes a bed with an air-circulation headboard for the sick room at the École Nationale Professionelle at Metz; develops the famous metal curtain wall for Buc Aviation Club with Eugene Beaudouin and Marcel Gabriel Lods, and with those architects designs a prototype weekend house
1937	Designs a model bathroom with Le Corbusier and Jeanneret for the World's Fair
1939	Completes Maison du Peuple, Clichy, designed in collaboration with Beaudouin and Lods; receives many commissions for school furniture; receives a patent for a portable house; manufactures 800 prefabricated huts for the French army; constructs weekend residence on stilts

1940–1944	Active member of the Résistance
1941	Designs portable housing with Lods
1944	Makes more than 110 prefab houses for homeless families in Lorraine and the Vosges
1944–45	Serves as mayor of Nancy
1945	Creates adjustable armchair out of sheet and tubular steel
1946	Makes furniture for students' rooms at the University of Nancy; designs prefab houses for Le Corbusier's Unité d'Habitation in Marseilles
1947	Opens new factory in Maxéville
1948	Manufactures desks made out of tubular steel and wood with Formica
1950	Designs with Le Corbusier a staircase and kitchens for the Cité Radieuse in Marseilles; manufactures Antony-style armchairs for the University of Strasbourg; receives the Chevalier de Légion d'Honneur
1953	Majority shares in the atelier acquired by Aluminum Français, which reorganizes the factory; Prouvé resigns
1954	Builds his own family house in Nancy; establishes design studio in Paris
1955–56	Founds Jean Prouvé Constructions
1956	Builds house in Paris for Abbé Pierre
1963	Wins Auguste Perret prize from the International Union of Architects
1964	Receives retrospective exhibition at the Musée des Arts Decoratifs in Paris
1971	Heads jury judging the design competition for the Centre Georges Pompidou
1984	Dies March 23 in Nancy

INDEX

| 96 |